SEARCHING AMERICAN LAND AND DEED RECORDS

SEARCHING AMERICAN LAND AND DEED RECORDS

By
FRAN CARTER

AGLL
Bountiful, Utah
1996

American Genealogical Lending Library
P.O. Box 329, Bountiful, UT 84010-329

Printed in the United States of America
99 98 97 96 8 7 6 5 4 3

ISBN 0-945433-29-8

CONTENTS

LAND OWNERSHIP SYSTEMS

Property was important to our ancestors. Historically, land ownership was one of two main reasons our ancestors came to the new world or migrated west. These were the right to own land and religious freedom. Probably the best kept of all land records and the most used for genealogical research are the *property records.* These most detailed documents are similar in most states.

It is difficult to prove relationships using only birth, marriage and death records in the United States because of the relatively late date most states required official registration of vital records. Land and deed records give us the substitutes for birth, marriage and death information in places and during times when other records may not exist.

Land and deed records become most important for us to not only <u>know</u> about, but to learn how to <u>find</u> and <u>use</u> effectively. These records contain information we need to unlock the doors from one generation to another and to prove relationships. The following information may lead us through the sometimes complicated documents created when property was purchased, changed hands, or was sold.

Searching land and deed records requires innovation, curiosity, creativity, and persistence. We must learn to be detectives when we are searching for our ancestors. In addition to these traits we need a knowledge of these *vitally important* record systems and how they function.

Sometimes our ancestors lived on the frontier. If a couple married and a ceremony was performed, it *might* have been noted in government or church records. If a couple had a child and it lived, the parents were grateful. However, often the only record of births, marriages, and deaths was in the family Bible. When our ancestors died, no one besides friends and family would have been notified, *unless the deceased owned property.* Property ownership needed to be changed, thus land records are left.

Transfer of land ownership or usage was accomplished by one or more of the following ways:

- DESCENT: The land was passed from one generation to another by direct line of descent.
- WILL: New ownership could be specified in a will from a relative or friend.
- BUYING: Acquisition by purchase, barter, or trade.
- SELLING: Release of land to buyer.
- GIVING: Making a gift of land, usually to children.
- LEASING: Land rented to a person conditionally for a specific period of time. Ownership is retained but use of land is given to another.
- MORTGAGE: Buying on time. Once the buyer has met the agreed terms, ownership is transferred. If the terms are not met, the owner can reclaim possession of the property.
- PUBLIC SALES: Property is made available to the public, usually at a reduced price. This includes auctions, tax sales, repossessions, and government incentive programs.
- EROSION: Wearing away of land by water, wind, or ice.
- ADVERSE POSSESSION: Occupation of land without permission of the owner. The taking of property by force.

COLONIAL LAND DIVISION

The early settlers of colonial America settled land without concern for boundary lines or recorded deeds. With the new settlers came the need for some systematic form of identifying who owned land, where it was located, and a method of describing each piece of property. Historically, these first *deeds* described the land using natural features as boundaries. This system of measurement was practical, down-to-earth, and useful for the time and place in which it was used. It worked well until neighbors began to disagree.

The early, unsystematic settlement of a community land created great turmoil, to say the least. The first settlers took up land along the waterways. This provided them with water, transportation, and communication. The water was used for household purposes, irrigation, and transportation between settlements. As more settlers arrived, they found the leftover land to be swampy or with steep slopes and poor soil. Then the land boundaries became a real problem.

Land claims overlapped and errors were commonplace. Boundary mistakes naturally occurred as land passed through various owners and with environmental changes. Good friends, as Robert Frost pointed out, made good neighbors. In the case of land problems, these good neighbors could help clarify irregular boundaries.

There was one early custom which gives and idea of how carefully land measurement was watched. Each spring the neighboring land owners walked together around their lots of land. They agreed on any boundary changes, erosion problems, or natural disasters which might have changed since the previous spring. This assured that all owners agreed upon the boundaries.

Later generations abandoned this custom. Fences fell, trees were chopped down or were struck by lightning, lakes dried up, river banks shifted with floods or rain, or other natural disasters changed land boundaries. These occurrences resulted in boundary disputes. Disagreements began to be resolved with systematic surveys and measurment of land. Maps of the parcels (plats) were drawn and, most importantly, *recorded.*

New England States chose to divide the land into squares called *towns* and to break the squares up into *lots* or *sections.* One side effect of this system of dividing land was that it kept one person from gaining control of all the best land in any one area. Settlers had to take the good land with the bad with the lot drawing system.

CHARTERS

Charters were grants of land given to a person designated by the King of England to become a *Proprietor* by means of the granting of a *Charter.* Of course, these charters were granted mostly to the aristocracy or people in favor with the current King and his court. They were money makers for the grantees. The grants gave them a *Document of Original Title* to the land and the privileges of rulership over those purchasing the property. Once the site for a town was selected (usually where water was available), the town was formed and the governing body was put in place.

Some of these proprietors settled the towns themselves and in turn divided the land. Others sold the land which was granted to them to freemen for profit. Once the *Proprietor* had sold the land to a *freeman* a deed was granted. The town clerk recorded this transaction in the Town Minute Books. Some interesting and genealogically oriented information can be found in these Town Meeting or Minute Books. We might find births, deaths and marriages recorded in these unindexed volumes also.

When reference to *Charters* is found in the records, one might be warned there are other records in other places concerning the freemen and the proprietor. These records should be considered locators, and information as to the settlement dates and the identities of the founders should be able to be found.

The body which was selected to rule the town governed everything from attendance in church to the prices charged for crops and goods. They decided who could own land and how much. They accepted or denied petitions of men to become *freeman.* Only *freemen* could vote or own land.

A *freeman* was a man who had attained the age of consent and was accepted by these town officials. He was then ready to buy land and become a part of the general community. Age seemed to make little difference. Some men have been made *freemen* as young as age 18 and others were acknowledged as late as age 30.

ESTABLISHMENT OF TOWNS

The town clerk and the officers of the town who were elected and appointed were the governing body over the new settlers. Sometimes there were not enough citizens living within a town (or township) to hold a court. If this happened, the court function was set up on a county basis with several towns or townships being assigned to a specific district. Thus, if we cannot find a town record we should look for a county or district recording of land and deed transactions.

These Town Courts or Councils could be quite adamant. If one did not like the way a vote was decided they could petition a *General Court* created by districts. As the New England town Council system grew it was guided under what we call the *State Land* system. This simply meant the state had jurisdiction over the land it owned. The Public Domain system is a Federal Government controlled system. The Public Domain System will be discussed later in this book.

As the District System evolved, two members from each town were selected to represent their town (and its people) in general court. This District system eventually evolved into our present legislature.

Towns are mentioned extensively in early New England Records. Remember that an entire area would be called a *Town.* A town was roughly three to six miles in dimension and measured in irregular boundary lines. An ordinary map may not show the name of a township, but will show the towns. The towns encompassed many miles, yet had only a small section of houses which we think of possibly as the town or village. Houses were located within the village and the farming was accomplished with in the outer area.

In the New England area the people set up a congregational type of government. Each town had its own church and town board. The officers for the town board were elected and a minister chosen. Thus each town was self-governed. The majority rule was used in all matters. If you were in the minority, your opinions were heard and you had the opportunity to voice those onions. And if you were in the minority and disagreed, there was plenty of land on the frontier. You either agreed with the majority, or moved to the frontier and created a new town and new governments. And thus our country grew.

The town commons, a section near the house area, was used to pasture livestock owned by anyone living in the village or town. Thus, you could see this system took a lot of community coordination. Everyone had to get along and work together. The land was divided and owned by individuals, and as a group.

Measurement was by metes and bounds following the irregular lay of land and can best be described by a drawing. Note the town or village is laid out it squares. The rest of the town was divided into town commons, farmland, pasture and unusual or swampy land. The lines follow the natural flow of nature. Rivers and creeks formed the boundaries.

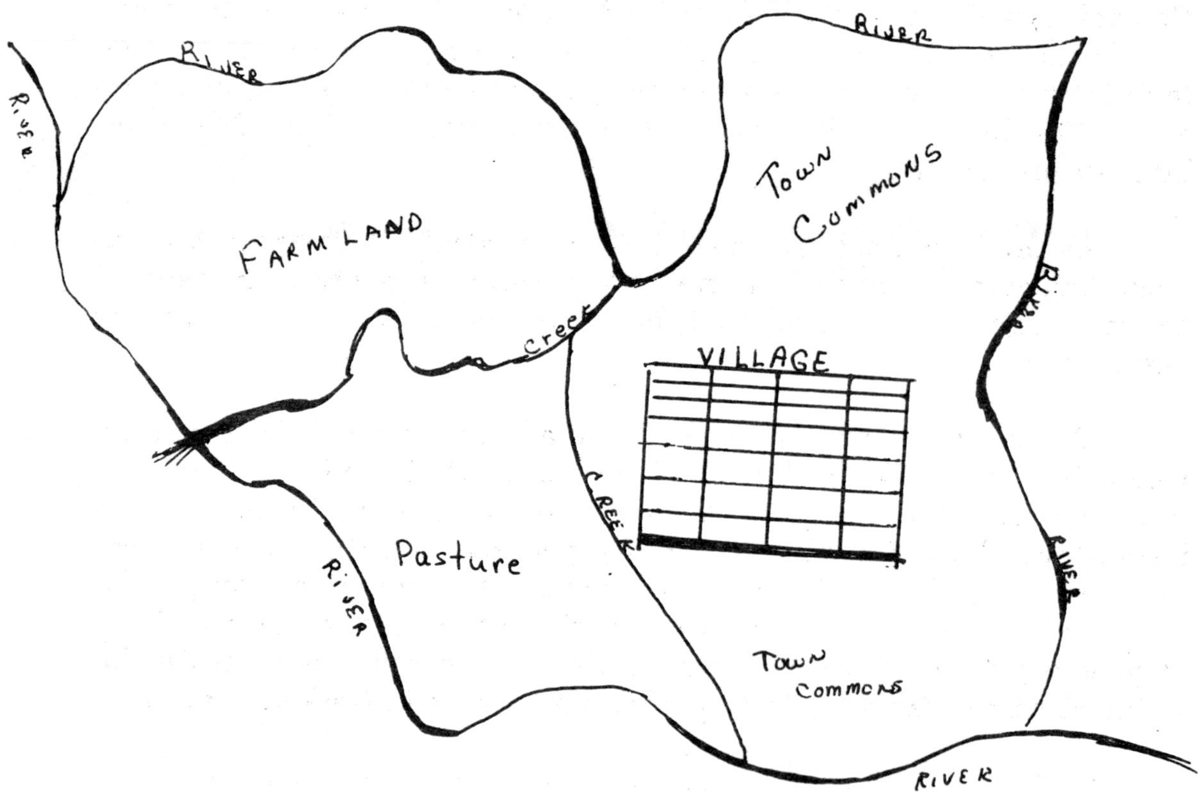

Locating an ancestor in one of the New England States land records will reveal many genealogical answers, such as when he moved to a new town, where he lived, his former residence, names of his children, his wife's family, his wife's maiden name, his age, and about his death.

STATE LAND STATES

State Land is a term which means the land was divided and measured in the metes and bounds measurement and governed by charters, proprietors and town rulings. The following states fit into this category of measurement and disbursement of land:

Connecticut

Connecticut also has several Probate Districts for each county and in some instances these records might be searched for your town or village recording of Land and Deed records.

Delaware

The Dutch West Indies Company adopted a Charter System in Delaware in 1629. The British took possession in 1664. Remember there were only three counties at this time in Delaware. Also be careful, records may be found in Philadelphia. Study the boundary changes.

Georgia

The basic rules for State Land states apply to Georgia.

Kentucky (From Virginia)

The basic rules for State Land states apply to Kentucky.

Maine (From Massachusetts)

The basic rules for State Land states apply to Maine.

Maryland

Maryland had a proprietary Government from 1634 to 1680, a Royal (King) Administration from 1690 to 1715, and a second proprietary government from 1716 to 1776 when Maryland became a state. After 1689, the Church of England established a "State Church" for a short period of time. Also, the boundary lines should be carefully watched. Search the Hall of Records in Annapolis, Maryland and the Land Office Records in Annapolis for Land and Deed records.

**Independent City: Baltimore*

Massachusetts

The basic rules for State Land states apply to Massachusetts.

New Hampshire

Deeds prior to 1770 are filed under the state jurisdiction and may be located in Concord, New Hampshire.

New Jersey

Records differ for this state from most of the other thirteen colonies. A proprietary colony with private titles to land for the benefit of private owners existed. The office of proprietors of Eastern New Jersey Division is in Perth Amboy, New Jersey. For West Jersey, the concessions and agreements of proprietors, freeholders and inhabitants is in Burlington, New Jersey.

New York

In 1664, the Duke of York took over this previously ruled Dutch colony. From 1664 to the time of the Revolutionary War the records are a part of the State's holdings. Large acreages were sold after the Revolution to land speculators. They in turn sold this land to individuals, many on credit. Records can be found in the mortgage files within each individual county.

In the central region of New York State, near Chenango County was a military tract set apart for Revolutionary soldiers. Bounty Land Warrants were used to redeem this land. The records may be found at the State Library in Albany, New York.

Deeds for the state are incomplete before 1823. There was no law requiring recordings until this 1823 date. Thus Land and Deed records may be found in town records or county records before this date.

Townships for New York may have names without a village in the township with the same name. If your ancestor states that he lived in a specific town, he was probably referring to the name of the township and not the city or village. So, be careful of this possibility.

North Carolina

It was a custom in North Carolina for a man to take his land grant and have a record made in the County Deed Books, thus many of the early records will also be recorded in the local courts.

Pennsylvania

The Land Office at Harrisburg has Documents of Original Title and Patent books. Surveyors' books are unindexed. Civil control over land records did not begin until 1885.

Rhode Island

For early land and deed records a normal rule should apply. Be aware of the Baptist infiltration and influence on land and deed records.

South Carolina

Early deeds until 1777 might be located in Charleston, South Carolina. The records in three of the six *districts* have been burned or destroyed. From 1798 to the present deeds are recorded by county.

Tennessee (From North Carolina)

The basic rules for State Land states apply to Tennessee.

Texas

The basic rules for State Land states apply to Texas.

Vermont

Records for early Vermont should be searched by probate districts first, then townships. Vermont was divided into probate districts with the names of townships fitting into the district system. All deeds are recorded by townships. Be aware that each Vermont

County has as many as two probate districts. A Works Progress Administration (W.P.A.) index was recorded for these districts and could be most helpful in finding which district your town or township might be.

Virginia

The first land grants were the Virginia Company of London, England which began with a charter from 1606 to 1624. Be aware of the headright system of obtaining lands, which meant a defined amount of acreage granted for each person brought into the country to settle. Some mention wives, relatives and servants. These relationships might be found in these headrights.

Independent Cities:

Alexandria, Bristol, Buena Vista, Charlottesville, Clifton Forge, Covington, Danville, Falls Church, Fredricksburg, Hampton, Harrisonburg, Hopewell, Lynchburg, Martinsville, Norfolk, Petersburg, Portsmouth, Radford, Richmond, Roanoke, South Norfolk, Staunton, Virginia Beach, Warwick, Waynesboro, Williamsburg, and Winchester.

West Virginia (From Virginia)

The basic rules for State Land states apply to West Virginia.

Most of these states or commonwealths, as some are called, follow common patterns of recording births, deaths and marriages as well as land and deed records in their land and deed books. Some states have unusual records. It should be noted that these do not follow the usual patterns.

There are 29 Independent Cities within the United States which have complete jurisdiction over their land, deed, and other records. They are set up much the same as the county governments and maintain their records in much the same manner. In addition to the independent cities listed above, St. Louis, Missouri is also an independent city.

PUBLIC DOMAIN STATES

Land owned by the United States government is referred to as *Public Domain.* After winning independence from England, the land was transferred from foreign governments and from the individual states to the United States. There are thirty states which have public domain lands:

Alabama
Alaska
Arizona
Arkansas
California
Colorado
Florida
Idaho
Illinois
Indiana
Iowa
Kansas
Louisiana
Michigan
Minnesota
Mississippi
Missouri
Montana
Nebraska
Nevada
New Mexico
North Dakota
Ohio
Oklahoma
Oregon
South Dakota
Utah
Washington
Wisconsin
Wyoming

From the beginning of this new Public Domain land distribution (1776 or so) until about 1812, the disposition or sale of these Public Domain lands were handled directly through the offices of the Secretary of the Treasury and the Registrar of the Treasury. In April of 1812 Congress approved a new office designated to care for Public Domain Land distribution called *The General Land Office.* This governmental agency was under the leadership of the Treasury department. In the original setting up of this system regional offices were opened as the need arose or as settlers began to populate specific districts. These offices helped the settlers handle the purchases and recording of their deeds.

When all, or almost all, of the land in the area was taken up (or sold), the general land office closed and new ones opened. Buyers of this land fell into different categories and will be discussed later. Once the final paper work was completed in the General Land Office, the documents were sent to the main headquarters in Washington D.C. A *final certificate* was issued which stated all the requirements had been met and a full deed would be presented to the purchaser. This process could have been a military grant, cash, or a mortgage. Whatever the initial process was, the procedure remained the same.

Warrants were issued permitting an applicant for land to locate or isolate a specified number of acres of public domain land. These were issued to anyone qualifying under various warrant acts. Many who qualified for a warrant under the various acts may never have applied for their warrant.

A person presenting a warrant to the *District Land Office* then asked for a *Patent* to be issued for a specific tract of land. Or, he could sell his warrant to someone else who might use it to obtain land *script* could also be presented in exchange for the title to a specific amount of land. Sound complicated? The terminology may be a bit different, but we can learn to understand the language fairly easily once we use it in our research.

By 1776, our new Congress had begun to create a National Land Policy. After all, they had to devise some way to handle and to dispose of the western lands they had just acquired when we gained our independence. The disposal of these land demanded quick action. Much land had been promised to revolutionary soldiers for their service in lieu of cash payments. And, a source of income was needed for the coffers of a newly founded government. A land policy which was understandable to the common people was necessary. It had to be designed quickly and it had to be efficient.

The *Old Northwest Territory* (all lands West and North of the Ohio River) was opened for settlement in the late 1700s. The solution of land division which the new Government devised was called *"The Land Ordinance Act of1785"* and has become otherwise known as the *"Township and Range Survey System."* Today we call the system *"The United States Public Land Survey System."*

The first step taken was to set up an initial point from which to begin measurement. *Parallel* and *Meridian* points were determined by a field survey. The *Parallel* line is called the *Baseline* from which to start measuring. The intersecting *Meridian* line is called the *Principal Meridian* line. When drawn on a map range lines began on the Meridian points at six mile intervals; township lines were surveyed along the parallel lines at six mile intervals. These six mile by six mile squares were called *Townships.* This set up our current survey system.

PUBLIC DOMAIN LAND RECORDS

The United States Government acquired large amounts of land from 1803 to 1867 which were surveyed and disbursed through the Public Domain Land Offices. The following were some of the large acquisitions of this period:

1803 Louisiana Purchase of 500,000,000 acres
1819 Florida
1846 Oregon, Washington and Idaho
1853 Southern Arizona, Gadsden Purchase
1867 Alaska

The measuring of this land under the Public Domain Land system has evolved into what we call the *Rectangular System,* using the Section, Township and Range method of measurement.

Some of the early records of the disposition of land to our ancestors can be found in a series of books entitled *Land Entry Papers.* These papers cover the years from 1800 to 1908 and are arranged by state. There is no master index. The land entry papers are filed by Range, Township, Section, or by a fraction of a section. Every name indexes beginning in 1908 and thereafter can be found alphabetically in these Land Entry Papers.

Much of the land in the United States is still owned by the federal government. Title of this land is gained by purchase, condemnation, gift, or exchange. These properties are called *Acquired Lands.* These acquired lands can be sold by the government to the general public.

THE PROCESS OF OBTAINING LAND TITLES

The paper flow created when land was purchased under the Public Domain System of distribution created documents of interest to the genealogist. Understanding this process, and realizing each step created a different set of papers, becomes most important.

File And Enter Papers (Staking A Claim)

Entry Books were established which contain abstracts of the Patent or Grant. The original entry records in the Public Domain records are housed in the Federal

Land Office. When a territory was opened a Land Office was created and all transactions were executed in this office. When all, or almost all, of the land had been granted the Land office closed and the records were transferred to the National Land Office. As time passed these old Land Grants were transferred to the National Archives.

Land Surveyed

After an *Entry* or *Claim* was filed, the second step was to initiate a Survey. This process was where the land was legally described. Surveys were not always recorded, but most were. These descriptions show the names of the applicants and the date it was filed. At the time the survey was completed a *Plat Map* was created (some of these also have the names of the settlers on them). These records were also housed with the General Land Office records.

Prove Up Terms

The Land Acts or Laws stated certain requirements must be met to obtain possession of land. It was up to the settler to fulfill these requirements before the land could belong to him - according to the law. This law of settlement varies from time to time and should be studied before a search is begun. The Prove Up Terms were the guidelines for the settler to follow.

Patent Or Grant Issued (Also Called The First Deed)

After the claim had been staked, the land had been surveyed, and the terms were met, the settler or tenant was given a *Patent or Grant*. This was the first paper which indicated they actually owned the land.

Transfer Of Title

After the settler had obtained his *Patent or Grant,* he was then free to sell all or part of his land. The title would then be transferred to the new owner and be recorded at a local county court. Some settlers after receiving their original *Patent or Grant* took them to the court house and registered them there in their own name. But if you are searching county records and cannot find the original purchase of the land, and the area was newly settled, at least suspect that the title was originally gained from the Public Domain System and would be recorded at the federal level of recording.

HOMESTEADING

The word "Homestead" may be one of the most misused words in family history study. We hear, " Our folks homesteaded out here in 1830." And yet the *Homestead Act* was not passed until 1862. The word was used synonymously with settlement and can often throw us off track in our search.

The Homestead Act was passed in 1862. It allowed any citizen or intended citizen who would settle the land a free quarter section beginning January 1, 1863. From 1863 to 1868, Minnesota attracted the most land seekers. Kansas and Nebraska led from 1869 to 1879. In the 1880's Dakota Territory surpassed all others.

By the Taylor Grazing Act of 1934 and its later amendments Congress virtually halted further homesteading except in Alaska, where free land continued to be available. The act provided that the Grazing Service was to administer and lease to stockmen all the remaining public lands.

There is still, however, land available for claiming in some states. One parcel of 100 acres was recently claimed in the Commonwealth of Kentucky. Of course, there was no road to this acreage, nor any place on it where one could stand flat-footed. But it was taken up, and filed in a proper manner and is currently being lived on by a family of five. Final papers are soon to be filed after a five-year residency and improvement requirements have been met.

The rules of homesteading vary from time to time. Included here are the rules for the State of Oregon for the late 1800s.

- No person who is the owner of more than 160 acres of land in any state or territory can acquire any right under the Homestead Act.

- A man must be at least 21 years of age to make an entry unless married or the head of a family.
- A married woman has no right of homestead. A deserted wife can make a *homestead entry.*
- A single woman over 21 years of age has the right to make an entry.
- A single woman does not forfeit her homestead entry by marriage if thereafter she continues to comply with the law as to residence, improvements, and cultivation. But a husband and wife cannot hold separate *homestead entries* and prove both.
- Widows or children of a homesteader are not required to reside on their homestead after the death of their husband or father, but must continue to cultivate by agent or otherwise. A widow can enter a homestead in her own right while cultivating that of her husband, in which event she must actually reside on the land entered in her own name.
- Homestead entries cannot be made for more than 160 acres.
- Five years residence from date of entry is required on homesteads for perfecting title, except for sailors or soldiers of the late war may apply at the time of residence, the period of their military service. But in all cases, there must not be less than 1 year actual residence on, and improvement of, the land.
- After 14 months of residence on a homestead the entry may be commuted, if desired, by paying $ 2.50 per acre if with the railway grant, 40 miles each side of the center of said tract, or pay $ 3.50 per acre if outside the said limit. Then the government will give them a patent.
- Any person who entered less than 160 acres of land as a homestead may then enter enough additional land which, added to the amount originally entered, would not exceed 160 acres.
- It is necessary to appear in person at the Land Office when making an entry of homestead lands.

Land Office fees when application was made for homestead entry were:

$14.00	for 160 acres
$13.00	for 120 acres
$ 7.00	for 80 acres
$ 6.00	for 40 acres

RECORDS FROM THE BUREAU OF LAND MANAGEMENT

Many records are kept by the Bureau of Land Management. These include homestead papers, selected tract books and copies of patents, and modern maps. The addresses of the various bureaus, their locations, and the states they cover follow:

- Bureau of Land Management, Eastern States
  7450 Boston Blvd.
  Springfield, VA 22153
  (Alabama, Alaska, Florida, Illinois, Indiana, Iowa, Louisiana, Michigan, Minnesota, Mississippi, Missouri, Ohio)

- Bureau of Land Management, *Alaska*
  Box 13, 701 C Street
  Anchorage, AK 99513

- Bureau of Land Management, *Arizona*
  2400 Valley Bank Center
  Phoenix, AZ 85073

- Bureau of Land Management, *California*
  Federal Bldg., Rm. E 2841
  2800 Cottage Way
  Sacramento, CA 95825

- Bureau of Land Management, *Colorado*
  1037 Twentieth Street
  Denver, CO 80202

- Bureau of Land Management,
  P.O. Box 30157
  Billings, MT 59107
  (Montana, North Dakota, South Dakota)

- Bureau of Land Management, *Nevada*
  300 Both Street
  Reno, NV 89520

- Bureau of Land Management
  P.O. Box 1449
  Santa Fe, NM 87501
  (New Mexico, Oklahoma, Texas)

- Bureau of Land Management
  P.O. Box 2965
  Portland, OR 97208
  (Oregon, Washington)

- Bureau of Land Management, *Utah*
  136 E. South Temple
  Salt Lake City, UT 84111

- Bureau of Land Management
  P.O. Box 1828
  Cheyenne WY 82001
  (Wyoming, Kansas and Nebraska)

To obtain homestead papers, the legal description of the land which includes section, township, range, and legal subdivision should be provided when requesting copies of papers in the *Patent Case Files* of the National Archives. This description can be obtained from the recorder of deeds of the county in which the land is located. Send this legal description to the Bureau of Land Management for copies of the Patent.

Once the patent is received, write to the National Archives, Reference Branch, General Archives Division, Washington, DC 20408 to obtain a copy of the homestead papers issued. Include:

- Name of person filing patent
- Legal description of land
- Patent number
- Date of patent
- Land office which issued the papers.

For states east of the Mississippi plus the states of Louisiana, Arkansas, Missouri, Iowa and Minnesota, the Bureau of Land Management has tract books and copies of patents. A patent is a grant made by the government to an individual conveying a fee simple title to public lands.

When the field office had finished their duties of disposing of most of the land within their jurisdiction the office was closed and the records were sent to Washington, D.C. The subsequent transfer of these records was accomplished and we can currently locate them at:

Eastern States Office
Bureau of Land Management
7450 Boston Blvd.
Springfield, VA 22153

The records found here include Surveys, Township Plat Maps and Survey Notes. These records might include:

Settler's name(s)
Activities during the time acquiring land
Homestead acts
Timber culture acts
Stock raising acts
Cash entries
Railroad lands
Speculator company records
Home lots records

The original entry books of the land office might contain:

Legal Descriptions
Names of applicants
Migratory groupings
Proof of residence
Patent Number

The Bureau of Land Management is also the principal mapping agency of the country. Maps come in all sizes, shapes, descriptions and colors. Systematic state maps are available for most Western States in the form of color quadrangle maps. The colors were used to distinguish various classes of public lands. Some are large scale and some are small scale maps. Maps should be sought after in your search for any land and deed information.

THE AMERICAN STATE PAPERS, 1789-1838

***The American State Papers* is a set of books which contain information about Federal Land transfers of title from the Government to another party. The first edition of this series contains 38 volumes and covers the follow categories.**

1. Foreign Relations (6 vols.)
2. Indian Affairs (2 vols.)
3. Finance (5 vols.)
4. Commerce & Navigation (2 vols.)
5. Military Affairs (7 vols.)
6. Naval Affairs (4 vols.)
7. Post Office Department (1 vol.)
8. Public Land Disposal (8 vols.)
9. Claims, Private Land claimed by individuals (1 vol.)

Each of these volumes is indexed individually. Categories 8 and 9 are indexed separately in a publication called *Grass Roots Of America, A Computerized Index to the American State Papers: Land Grants and Claims.* If you do not find these books in the genealogical section of your library, search in the reference section. Most moderate sized libraries have the *American State Papers.*

Federal transfers of land records transfer title (ownership) from the United States government to another party. All

subsequent records would be found recorded at the county level of government.

For further research, contact:

General Branch NNFG
Civil Archives Division,
National Archives and Records Administration
Washington, DC 20409

MILITARY BOUNTY LANDS

Military Bounty Land Warrants were issued under Congressional Acts for services rendered to the United States for the Revolutionary War and went through at least 1855 for other wars. These Warrants and Bounties were filed either by number, the number of acres granted, the legal description of the land, or any combination of the three.

Indexes exist for most Bounty Land Warrants for the Revolutionary War and the War of 1812. A warrant number was issued for each applicant. After the warrant was surrendered, entered into the records, and finalized, it was sent to the Federal Land Office. We might search for these records in Land Office Records and/or the National Archives. Land entry papers and abstract books for all Federal Public Domain States and the record copies for patents and central office tract books for the Western part of the United States are housed at the National Archives.

Warrants issued under acts of 1847 through 1855 are not indexed. Many acts by both federal, state and local governments regarding military grants of land should be studied. An example of one of the acts and how it affected participants is *The Settler Armed Occupation Act.*

> This act was issued by the Federal Land Office and provided for *armed* occupation and settlement of unsettled parts of the country. It was passed by the U.S. Congress 4 August 1842. The act provided that any person *being the head of a family, or a single man over eighteen years of age and able to bear arms* could settle, erect a house, clear and cultivate at least five acres of land, and live there for four years. Then he would be entitled to a quarter section of land (160 acres).

The purpose was obvious. War with the Indians was long and costly in both lives and money. Before the first of April 1842, a total of 1,466 soldiers and several hundred volunteers and settlers had lost their lives in Indian raids.

The *Settler Armed Occupation Act* did not prove to be satisfactory in that it was difficult to provide the proper "proofs" for final title. In later years, the Homestead Act of 1862 learned much from the failure of the Settler Armed Occupation Act and rectified most of the errors. When this 1862 act went into action it was set up more effectively and efficiently.

DEEDS

DEFINITION

A *Deed* is an instrument, written in proper legal form, which conveys property from one owner to another. Deeds show ownership of *real property* as well as *personal property* which may be recorded in the legal proceedings of a specific jurisdiction. Today, a deed must be in writing to comply with local laws. Historically, the *deed* developed from early times when it was known as "livery and seizin."

The story goes: The buyer and the seller of a piece of property, along with their individual witnesses, would go to the property being sold. The seller would scoop up a clod of earth from the ground, or break a branch from a tree while formally making the statement, "In the name of Seizena," and declare he was selling that land to the buyer. Stated in front of witnesses, it was the only formal act made and nothing more was recorded. We can see why this didn't work for very many years.

The first written instruments were committed to paper, witnessed, and then physically torn apart. The fitting of these two pieces of paper together was proof of the "contract" being valid. Property records are similar in almost every state. Federal and state laws have evolved, changed, and become as universal as they can be made.

The function of any deed is to transfer property from one person to another. But do not expect all deeds to be alike. Each clerk in each county seemed to have his own system, his own phrases, and his own way of writing. The very first time you locate a deed involving an ancestor, read through it carefully. The handwriting and terms used may be difficult to understand. After the deciphering the first one, each succeeding one will seem easier to read until you will become quite proficient with the writing and the terms used.

The opening words of most deeds read, "*This indenture ...*" This phrase simply means "this paper, this instrument, or this document."

Land And Deed Book 1845-1848
Madison County, Kentucky
page 487-488

I, J M Shackelford, Clerk of the County Court of Madison County Kentucky do certify that this deed of Conveyance was aforesaid and to me given for record on the 3rd day of March 1846, and the same delivered and duly recorded in my office. J M Shackelford CCC

This indenture made and entered into this first day of September 1828 by and between Ebenezer Titus and Dorothy his wife, late Dorothy Lee, James Stephenson and Polly his wife, late Polly Lee, Noah Lee, Sally West, late Sally Lee, Richard Lee, David Lee, Thomas Lee, Grissom Lee, Hezekiah W Wright and Delight his wife, late Delita Lee, James Lee, David W Dalton and Margaret his wife, late Margaret Lee, Irvine Lee, Preston Forrest and Lucinda his wife, late Lucinda Lee, Joel Todd and his Children to wit: Martha Ann Todd, Mary Jane Todd, Elizabeth Boatman, late Elizabeth Todd, John Todd, Irvine Todd, Newton Todd, Amanda Todd, Lucinda Todd and Joel Todd Jr, heirs and legal representatives of Nancy Todd, deceased, late Nancy Lee, and Robert Belsha, Dorothy Belsha. By Kiziah Cook a Commissioner appointed by a decree of the Madison County Circuit Court in the case of Richard Lee's heirs of the first part and Thomas McGuire and Ann his wife late Ann Lee of the second part. That whereas by the decree aforesaid in the causes aforesaid the same commissioner was directed to survey and divide the last of Richard Lee, deceased, estate, equally in value among all his heirs, his assignees done as is his judgment as much right. The land is in Madison County on the Brushy fork of the Silver Creek containing 352 aces as the part of said land laid off by them and hereby conveys in 23 acres marked on the commissioners report and returned to the aforesaid lot 13 bounded as follows, to wit:

Beginning at a stake and pointers in a drain corner to the north 12, and on the east line of the 352 acres, thence with the said line 21 poles to 3 black locusts on a hillside, corner of lot number 1 with a line of same west 171 poles to a stake and 3 white oak on the west of the 352 acres, thence with the line north east 21 poles to a large black oak thence with a line of southwest 12 east 171 poles to the beginning.

Now the parties of the first part by the commissioner aforesaid hereby conveys to the parties of the second part aforesaid all the titles and interests in said 23 acres of land which they have devised from their ancestor Richard Lee deceased, and the appurtenances belonging thereto. To have and to hold the same to these two parties of the second part and their heirs forever. The said commissioner is not to be liable in any event whatsoever. In testimony whereof the grantors aforesaid by the said commissioner hereunto set their hands and seals.

The above instrument was signed by all 36 people named in the deed, even the underage children. It is important when analyzing the above deed to note that there was obviously a disagreement among the parties since they are all related. [This researcher later proved all the relationships.] More records to search are indicated. But this was found in the Deed Books and was not an unusual find. Deed books answer many of our genealogical questions.

Just remember, deeds are copied. The original is always given to the owner of the property. The clerk makes a copy of the deed in a book called Deed Book [followed by a number or letter] such as Deed Book C or Deed Book 2.

TYPES OF DEEDS

Deeds are the instruments which transfer property ownership from one person or entity to another. There are various types of deeds, some do not have the word "Deed" in the title but they are still deeds or instruments which transfer title.

DEEDS IN FEE SIMPLE: Deed granting absolute ownership, but with no guarantee.

QUIT CLAIM DEEDS: Deeds which release whatever claim to title or right to title the owner held, whether valid or not. No guarantee is offered.

DEEDS OF GIFT, OR DEEDS OF LOVE: Deeds which transfer title without reciprocal or market price value or consideration (money) except perhaps "*love and affection.*" These are found in deed books and *suggest*, but don't guarantee, blood relationships. The consideration (price) may never be mentioned, or if it is, it may be small.

WARRANTY DEEDS: Warrant means to guarantee. Adding the "-y" to the end of the word means to officially guarantee. A Warranty Deed offers an assurance by the seller of the property that the property is as represented or promised. This suggests that the owner or seller of the property has the absolute right to transfer title to the property.

SHERIFF'S OR COMMISSIONER'S DEEDS: The Sheriff or Commissioner of any county has the power to sell land for unpaid or back taxes. They have the legal right to grant the deed in the absence of the owner and are called *Sheriff's Deeds.* The deeds are indexed under the sheriff's name.

WILL DEEDS: A deed which transfers property may be written as a will. It would be recorded in the Deed Books and may have been left out of the will books in any given county. They read like wills, but qualify in the courts as *Will Deeds.*

DEED OF TRUST: A mortgage arrangement which allows a third party to hold the deed until a buyer has paid the debt incurred. The deed is listed under the name of the buyer in the deed books and in the mortgage books. There should be an entry in the Mortgage Release books recorded when the debt is paid.

DEED OF ACQUITTANCE: A deed by which additional acreage is transferred or sold to the original patent owner and it has been found, by survey, that the patent land had more acreage than was originally thought. These are rare, but when found the explanation makes sense so the acreage would be listed correctly in the full deed.

DEED OF AGREEMENT: This deed is concerned with the sale of *personal property* as well as real property. It gives land to persons who agree to take care of the original land owner, the grantor, for the remainder of the grantor's life. What an insurance policy!

DEED OF CONVEYANCE: The transfer of ownership of property or ownership of a land warrant. These are early historic deeds and not easily found.

DEED OF DECREE: A deed showing property sold without monetary payment.

DEED OF PARTITION: Property which has been deeded by those holding joint ownership.

DEED OF SEPARATION: Made through a third party acting as a trustee, provision is made by a husband for separation from his wife and her separate maintenance.

DEED POLL: One person *only* is obligated to fulfill the terms of the deed.

EXECUTOR'S DEED: A deed administered by an executor of an estate.

INDENTURE DEED: A deed between two or more parties conveying real estate. Originally made in two parts so that it could be separated by tearing a jagged line and matched later. One of the earliest types of deeds.

POWER OF ATTORNEY DEEDS: Usually these deeds come out of the Probate Courts. Rights are granted by one person to act in behalf of another person. Especially used when the heirs have moved out of the area. They give their Power of Attorney to someone to transfer the title of land (usually land which they have inherited). These deeds might be listed under the name of the attorney or appointed person who acted in their place in the indexes. Be careful and search thoroughly for these deeds.

MARRIAGE CONTRACTS: Marriage Contracts may be found in land and deed records. These were used when a widow or widower remarried, and they wished their respective families by a previous marriage to have complete rights to their property acquired during the earlier marriage(s).

VOTING POLL DEEDS: In some areas, only those owning land were permitted to vote. Voting polls may be found in deed books. (In the New England States these may be found as *Freemen Lists.*)

BILLS OF SALE: **A slave may be bought and sold and listed in deed books. Deeds, or Bills of Sale, involving the sale of personal property can and are found in regular deed books.**

The following deed is an example of what can be found in a Deed Book other than land. This deed conveys two cows.

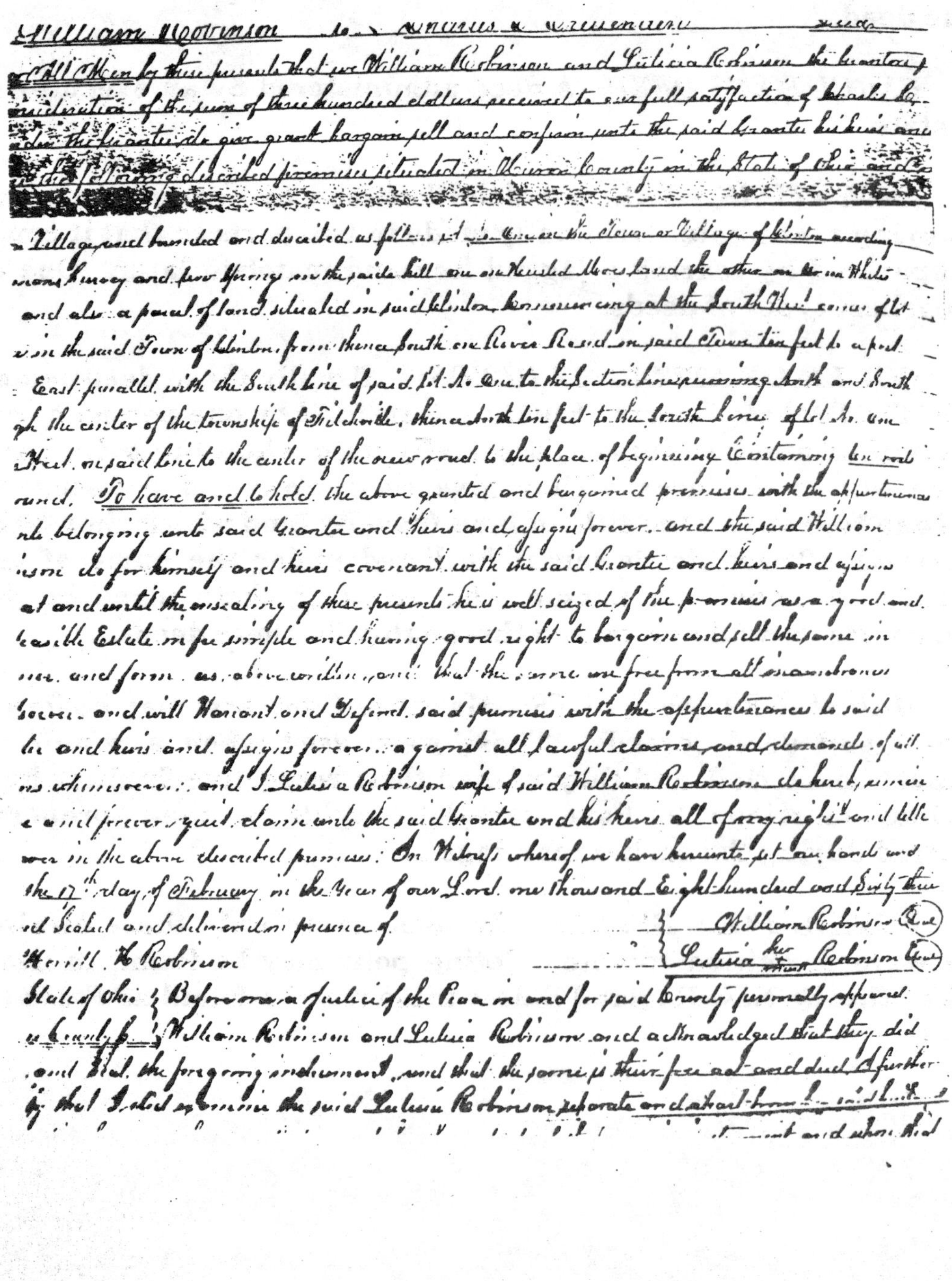
William Robinson to [illegible] Deed
All Men by these presents that we William Robinson and Lulicia Robinson the Grantors
[illegible] of the sum of three hundred dollars received to our full satisfaction of [illegible]
[illegible] the Grantee do give grant bargain sell and confirm unto the said Grantee his heirs and
[illegible] following described premises situated in [illegible] County in the State of Ohio and [illegible]
[illegible]
Village and bounded and described as follows [illegible] in the Town or Village of [illegible] according
[illegible] and two Springs on the said hill one on [illegible] land the other on [illegible] White
and also a parcel of land situated in said [illegible] commencing at the South West corner of lot
[illegible] in the said Town of [illegible] from thence South on River Road in said Town ten feet to a post
East parallel with the South line of said Lot No. One to the Section line running North and South
[illegible] the center of the township of [illegible] thence North ten feet to the South line of lot No. One
[illegible] on said line to the center of the new road to the place of beginning Containing ten rods
[illegible] To have and to hold the above granted and bargained premises with the appurtenances
[illegible] belonging unto said Grantee and heirs and assigns forever. and the said William
[illegible] do for himself and heirs covenant with the said Grantee and heirs and assigns
at and until the ensealing of these presents he is well seized of the premises as a good and
[illegible] Estate in fee simple and having good right to bargain and sell the same in
[illegible] and form as above written, and that the same are free from all incumbrances
[illegible] and will Warrant and Defend said premises with the appurtenances to said
[illegible] and heirs and assigns forever against all lawful claims and demands of all
[illegible] whomsoever. and I Lulicia Robinson wife of said William Robinson do hereby [illegible]
[illegible] forever quit claim unto the said Grantee and his heirs all of my right and title
[illegible] in the above described premises. In Witness whereof we have hereunto set our hands and
the 17th day of February in the Year of our Lord one thousand Eight hundred and Sixty three
[illegible] Sealed and delivered in presence of
William Robinson (Seal)
Lutisia her mark Robinson (Seal)
Merrill H Robinson
State of Ohio } Before me a Justice of the Peace in and for said County personally appeared
[illegible] County ss } William Robinson and Lutisia Robinson and acknowledged that they did
[illegible] the foregoing instrument, and that the same is their free act and deed, I further
[illegible] that I did examine the said Lutisia Robinson separate and apart from [illegible]
[illegible] and when [illegible]

ESSENTIALS OF A VALID DEED

The names of the parties involved

Consideration

Granting and Habendum Clause (conveys title)

Designation of Quantity of present interest transferred

Description of Property

Amount of Property being transferred

Legal Description

Signatures (all parties involved)

Recorded

Voluntary delivery and acceptance of all parties

NON-DEED ITEMS FOUND IN DEED BOOKS

Often, Deed Books contain much information other than land and deed records. In the early years of a county the tax structure had not yet provided enough revenue to purchase a variety of books for housing separate records. The following are a few items other than deeds which might be found recorded in these books.

POWER OF ATTORNEY: The appointment of an agent or agents to act instead of another person. These powers of attorney offer much genealogical information. May be found when one or more heirs of an estate have moved from an area and grant a "*power of attorney*" to sell land which they have received from a deceased relative.

BILLS OF SALE: Transferring property that is not real property. Slave records might be found in deed books.

LEASES: Long term leases, especially 99 year leases, are recorded in deed books. Especially those which permit building upon land when the land is not owned by the builder. This can be found when an owner does not want to sell the land, give clear title or when a governmental agency owns land which by law owns land which cannot be sold.

RELEASES or LEASE AND RELEASE: Historically this was a method of buying land to avoid paying English Court Fees. The land was leased for a period of time until all rights were finally purchased through a *release.* Early colonial records might contain these records, usually filed under *Lease and Release.*

PARTNERSHIPS: Partnerships in land ownership may be recorded in deed books even when they have nothing to do with land purchases or sales.

SLAVE MANUMISSIONS and SLAVE SALES: Slaves were considered property. As a slave was granted freedom the papers were filed in the land and deed records. As a slave was bought or sold the recording would be found in the land and deed books.

APPRENTICE PAPERS: Contracts with a person for a defined period of time which guaranteed that a person would be taught a trade and released with certain conditions are filed in land and deed books. Since this might be considered "property for years." the clerks recorded it in these records.

DEED REGISTRATIONS: Land is usually recorded under the names of the buyer and the seller. In these *Deed Registration* documents might also be found records recorded under the tract name or number. Today a housing development might be recorded under the developer's name. Historically, it might have been listed under "Borden's Tract," since a Mr. Borden bought the land, subdivided it, and sold it to individuals. These are called *Deed Registrations.*

DOWER RELEASE: In early deeds, the sale of land would not have been considered binding unless the wife also signed off her right to the property. By law, she was entitled to one-third of the property which her husband owned. This was called her *Dower Right.* The law specified that she must release these rights. Protocol said that three individuals would question her in privately with an officer of the court present. She was asked if any force, coercion, or threats were used to have her sign the papers. The recording of this instrument may have occurred the same day or within a few days after the sale of the property. It may be found within a few pages of the recording of the sale deed. The Dower Release gives valuable clues and may even list the wife's maiden name.

MARGINAL NOTES: Notes written in the margin of deeds offer many clues. Clerks used the margins to add notes to lead them to other records. There may be birth, death, and marriage records or information pertaining to the property being bought or sold. These notes were designed to give the clerk clues to follow and were not intended for historical reference.

INFORMATION TO EXTRACT FROM DEEDS

- ✍Name of Grantor and Grantee (Buyer and Seller)
- ✍Place of Residence (where they came from)
- ✍Consideration (Money, Love, Gift, etc.)
- ✍Description of Property (Long and Short Descriptions)
  - ✍ Number of Acres
  - ✍ Neighbors
  - ✍ Water Courses (Rivers, Creeks, etc.)
  - ✍ Metes and Bounds
  - ✍ Township and Range
  - ✍ Town or Village
  - ✍ County and Township
  - ✍ State
- ✍Current Place of Residence
- ✍Warrant (number)
- ✍Date of Document
- ✍Date of Recording
- ✍Chain Bearers (South, check for relationships)
- ✍Names of Witnesses
- ✍Signatures
- ✍Dower Releases (Check a few pages later than the deed)
- ✍Marginal Notes

Copy everything *exactly* as it is written on the deed. With any abbreviations, any wording, record them as you find them. Make your assumptions later. If Wm is found write Wm, not William.

INDEXES TO DEEDS

Indexes were prepared for the benefit of the county clerk, not the genealogist. We may find some of them to be incomplete. However, each courthouse has some sort of master index. The most common indexes are called *Grantee [Buyer] and Grantor [Seller] Indexes.* These indexes are usually arranged alphabetically and then chronologically.

Some indexes to land and deed records are very simple and have *all* names beginning with the letter "A" under "A" regardless of the second or following letters in the name. Looking through the entire list for a letter can take more time to locate an ancestor. Look through all the entries of a letter to find your ancestor's name. A list of some different types of indexes follows.

GRANTOR INDEXES index the Seller.

GRANTEE INDEXES index the Buyer.

DIRECT INDEXES index the Seller.

INDIRECT INDEXES index the Buyer.

CUMULATIVE DEED INDEXES are usually an alphabetical listing of all transactions by year or years.

RUNNING INDEXES are indexes which have all of the A's together, then all of the B's, etc., but are not indexed within the alphabetical listing.

PHONETIC INDEXES are spelled as they sound, thus recorded under the alphabetical listing, then by phonetic sound.

I know how exciting it is the first time you find the name you are searching for in an index, but *stop* right here and record the name and page numbers you are searching. Then continue on through the list for other transactions under the same name.

Look for *all* entries under any one name before searching the deed books themselves. The possibility exists that the deed transaction for which you are searching is not in the name of the ancestor for which you are searching. It may be in another name altogether.

> *Finding no probate packet for a specific family, we found a deed of purchase for my ancestor Miller Ross Thornton. He disappeared from census records after 1850. The Grantee/Grantor indexes were searched and the name was not found. Working later on collateral lines a daughter was found to have married a John Bullock. Researching these same indexes under the name Bullock Miller Ross Thornton's name appeared. The final distribution and sale of the property was listed under John Bullock. Each of the descendants of Miller Ross Thornton was identified and named, with addresses, and most importantly the name of all the grandchildren, children of a deceased daughter (my grandmother).*

When working in land and deed indexes, each index book should be examined first on the beginning page. There may be a key or a note to a system change. Each new clerk, as he took office, may have changed the indexing system. Also, Jr. and Sr. when found in land and deed records does not necessarily mean the father and the son. Historically it may have been someone of the same name, not necessarily related, living in the same area.

When you are told, " The courthouse burned," do not give up until you have done more investigating into the matter. Maybe it did burn. And maybe, just maybe, all the records were destroyed. But you can bet that the next day after the fire, officials began reconstructing those records. Land records were the basis of the county's taxes. The revenues from the taxes paid their salaries. Each land owner in the county was usually asked to come in and reregister their deeds. Thus when you hear the phrase, "the court house burned," think of the land and deed records first. They may go back to the time period needed.

Commercial companies have been providing books for county business since early times. One company from Ohio has had a patented indexing system since 1888 which is unusual. It is called the Cott System. In this system, common family surnames and family names are "set out" and others are in "mixed group" pages. To find the page on which your name is entered look first under the *Proper Prime* or Master Subdivision (the first letter of your surname).

Printed at the top of the column is a description to determine if your name is "set out." If your name is not listed, refer to the proper mixed group page. Groups start on the front sheet, right hand page and continue onto the back of the page. All this explanation above just means the Brown family may be "set out" on a separate page because there were so many of them.

Other references to the "mixed group" type of indexing might be the commercial entries such as the AAA (auto club) or WLS radio stations. There may be separate entry pages for these types of entries. Names beginning with numbers also fit into the special group class as well as Churches, Universities, Trustees, Cemeteries, Trustees of Cemeteries, Lodges, etc. In other words, if a school owned property, it might be in the mixed group form of indexing, under *Schools*.

All common names in the Cott System and varying active names might be "set out." Such as:

Saa- Sab - Sacad
Sae - Saf - Sag - Sah

HOW TO OBTAIN LAND AND DEED RECORDS

Each county within the United States has land and deed records. After all, these records are their tax base and thus kept current, efficient, effective, and easily accessed. Usually they are indexed in a similar manner. Thus once we learn about the system of indexing and the details for which we are searching, these records are fairly easily accessed.

They can be obtained by visiting or writing to a particular courthouse. Many of the county records have filmed by The Church of Jesus Christ of Latter-day Saints. These films can be viewed at your local Family History Center or the Family History Library in Salt Lake City, Utah.

PRINTED ABSTRACTS

Many counties, genealogical societies, and historians are printing early land and deed records for use in researching. These appear in book form, journals, quarterlies, and other publications.

Dedicated researchers are providing this service. The records are rapidly becoming more accessible. Always check first to see if an abstract form of early deeds has been printed. It may save time.

Printed abstracts of deeds often contain information on the buyer, seller, original owner, warrant number, certificate number, neighbors, and other pertinent information to help us in our research. Two entries are copied here as examples.

Deed Book One, Gibson County, Tennessee.

p. 260 #423, State of Tennessee, 13th District, by virtue of entry #603 dated 11 Dec. 1822, Founded on warrant #5065 issued by the Secretary of State of North Carolina on 6 October 1797 to the heirs of Bailey Anderson. Surveyed for the heirs of Bailey Anderson 640 acres. Henry County, Richland Creek, 1 range, 9 section, surveyed 12 June 1823 by Nathan G Pinson. SCC., Samuel Nelms, William Nelms, returned August 1823, from office 7 May 1823 by J C McLemore.

p. 263, #423 State of Tennessee, 13th District by virtue of entry #417 date 26 May 1821 founded on certificate #1802 issued by the Commissioner of West Tennessee to David Ross for 1148 acres dated 18 October 1820. Range 9 Section 8 Henry County in the Mississippi Bottom, begin on the bank of the river to the lines of McLemore and Lytle, Vaulx, surveyed 5 July 1823...

One might see from the above abstracts of land and deed records that further research could identify heirs, neighbors, military records, and other similar records useful to genealogists. The abstractors have taken information and condensed it into usable form. Each abstractor may identify information differently but the information is there to lead you to these and other original records.

COURT ORDER BOOKS

Colonial States usually kept good records. Many of the early land and deed records might be found in the Court Order books or the Court Minute books. Some have been lost, but those which do exist provide a colorful account of the lives and times of our

ancestors. Genealogical information may be extensive. They may contain land and deed records involved in the following types of actions, especially if there might have been a land dispute over title or boundary lines:

- **Names of plaintiffs or defendants**
- **Jury lists, judges, witnesses, legal representatives, etc.**
- **Types of cases and court actions**
- **Licenses**
- **Guardian appointments, approvals, reports etc.**
- **Bonds**
- **Powers of attorney**
- **Actions on land and deed problems**

GLOSSARY

TERMS USED IN LAND AND DEED RESEARCH

ABSTRACT: The summary or abridgment of a record. It should contain the same basic information in shorter form. A copy of pertinent information from a lengthy record.

ABSTRACT OF TITLE: A shortened version of all documents affecting the title of a tract of land. Including a listing of all actions, decrees, conveyances, written instruments, as well as all people who had dealings with a particular property, giving all information concerning the title of land.

ACCOUNT: Report of an administrator or executor of an estate which included the settlement and disbursement of property.

ACQUIRED LAND: Federal lands acquired by purchase, by condemnation, or by gift, which is under the jurisdiction of the public land laws.

ACRE: 43,560 square feet or 10 square chains of land.

ACRE-DALE: A common field in which several proprietors held an interest, not necessarily on an equal basis.

ACRE TAX: The English method of taxing land at a certain amount per acre.

ACTUAL GRANT: In Colonial America, a grant made by the English Crown.

AFFIDAVIT: A written document created while under oath before an officer of the court.

AGRARIAN: A person who favors an equal division of landed property. Or, a change in ownership of land.

ALIAS: An assumed name.

ALIENE: To transfer property, or title of property to another.

ALIENEE: The buyer, or person to whom the ownership of property is transferred.

AMERICAN STATE PAPERS: A set of books which contain various Private and Public land disposal lands by the Federal Government and individuals. There are nine categories covered in these books. Categories eight and nine deal with public land disposals and private land claims by individuals.

ANNO DOMINI: Latin term meaning "in the year of our Lord."

ANNUITY: A yearly, or annual payment.

ANTENUPTIAL CONTRACT: Special arrangements made by couples intending marriage regarding their estates. Especially designed for parents who have children by a previous marriage and are wishing to marry again. By which, they protect the first spouse's estate for their heirs.

APPEARANCE RECORD: A chronological record or docket of all cases coming into a court.

APPURTENANCES: Something added too a more important thing, such as a house or outbuildings added to land.

ARPENT: An old French land measurement of varying value, equal to approximately .84 acres; a linear measure equal to approximately 11.5 rods. Often used in Canadian land measurement.

ASSESSED VALUATION: Official value of property for the purpose of taxation.

ASSIGN: To transfer as a claim, or right, or property.

ASSIGNEE: A person to whom an assignment is made.

ATTEST: To bear witness. To affirm as true.

BASE LINE: The East-West line used for surveying within the Public Domain states.

BAYOU: A stream forming a sluggish and marshy outlet or inlet to a larger body of water.

BENEFICIAL OWNERSHIP: The use of property by a beneficiary even though he or she is not the legal owner of the property.

BLACK RENT: Rents paid in produce instead of money.

BOUNTY LAND: Public land awarded to soldiers for military service.

CARUCATE: A measure of land, as much as could be tilled with a team of 8 oxen in one year. (Early English, some early colonies)

CASH LAND: Public Domain land which was sold for cash.

CHAIN: A lineal measure of land 66 feet, 100 links of chain or 4 poles, and equal to 1/80 of a mile.

CHAIN OF TITLE: Successive conveyance of title to a certain piece of property starting with the patent or other original source and ending with the present day title holder.

CHAIN BEARER: A person hired to carry the chains for the person measuring land. Mostly southern measurements - be careful, these may be relationships.

COMMON PLEA: Civil action brought by one person against another. Usually referred to as a Court of Common Plea which hears cases of one person against another. Can be referred to in Land and Deed Records when there is a dispute.

CONSANGUINEOUS: Related by blood. This term may be found in early deeds.

CONSORT: Companion, wife or husband, spouse, mate.

CONTINGENT: In land records this means the rights to accrue on the happenings of a future event.

CONVEY: The transfer of title of property to another, by a written document such as a deed: To transfer ownership.

CONVEYANCE: A legal document by which the title of property or land is transferred.

CORDUROY ROAD: A road made of tree trunks laid across a swampy area. These roads may be mentioned in land and deed records as conscription roads. People paid toll by helping build a section of road.

CORSERIE: Buying and selling.

COUNTY: A local administrative subdivision of a state. Local governmental unit.

COURT OF OYER AND TERMINER: A criminal court held with the court of quarter sessions. Court which handled some land and deed disputes.

COURT WEEK: The week when a County Court was in session.

***DE ANNO IN ANNUM*:** Latin term meaning "from year to year."

DEED: A written document which conveys legal entitlement to property.

DEED OF AGREEMENT: Concerned with the sale of personal property, deeds land to persons who agree to take care of the grantor for the remainder of their lives.

DEED OF CONVEYANCE: Transfer of ownership of property and perhaps the ownership of a land warrant.

DEED OF DECREE: A document showing property sold without a monetary payment as consideration.

DEED OF PARTITION: Property deeded by those holding property jointly.

DEED OF SEPARATION: Through the medium of a third party acting as a trustee, this deed makes provision by a husband for separation from his wife and for her separate maintenance.

DEED OF TRUST: A Mortgage arrangement which allows for a third party to hold the deed until the buyer has paid his debt.

DEED POLL: One person only is obligated to fulfill the terms of this deed. They are sometimes used as voting registers.

DEFEASANCE: A collateral deed which, upon certain conditions, will make another deed null and void.

DEGREE OF RELATIONSHIP: The distance between two persons related by blood under Canon Law.

DEMISE: Death; Time of death.

DESCENDANTS: Offspring of a specific ancestor.

DEVISEE: Person to whom real property is given in a will.

DISPOSE: To assign, make over to, grant, or convey land.

DIVIDENT: Land divided and included in a patent or grant.

DONATION LANDS: Public lands donated or given to settlers for fulfilling certain specified requirements. Generally in exchange for military service. Notably Indiana and Texas, but other states have Donation lands.

DOWER: Provisions made from a husband's estate for the support of his widow and family. Usually 1/3 of the value of the real estate only.

DOWER RELEASE: An agreement which forfeited a wife's right to any of her deceased husband's land that he sold to another.

DOWER RIGHT: The right of a wife to at least 1/3 of the land her husband had at the time of their marriage or acquired during their marriage.

DRAUGHT: Land which had been surveyed and draughted (drafted) for which settlers drew lots.

EMINENT DOMAIN: Superior dominion of the sovereign power over property within a state: authorized it to appropriate all or any part of that land for public use. Reasonable compensation must be made.

ENTAIL: A restriction placed on how land could be passed on to descendants.

ENTAILED ESTATE: An estate limited in the manner that it can be transferred, such as allowing the estate to be inherited only by a specific line of descent, and preventing one from transferring it outside that line.

EQUITABLE OWNERSHIP: Benefits of real estate without actually being the owner named on the deed, such as a Trust.

EQUITABLE TITLE: The right of legal title upon fulfilling certain obligations such as a mortgage.

EQUITABLE REDEMPTION: Property in the processes of foreclosure, when one can regain land by paying the mortgage in full plus costs of foreclosure.

ESCHEAT: Land that reverts back to the government because no proven heirs could be found.

ESCROW: A document, instrument or payment held by a third party and delivered when the conditions of the agreement are met.

***EX CURIA*:** A Latin term meaning "out of court."

EXECUTOR DEED: A deed administered by an executor of an estate.

***EX FACTO*:** Latin term meaning "from, or by, the deed."

EX POST FACTO: A Latin term meaning "after the act."

FALLOW: Land which is plowed by not sowed to enrich the soil.

FEE: An estate completely owned by a person which can be sold or given as an inheritance by that person.

FEE SIMPLE: An inheritance having no conditions or limitations in its use.

FEE TAIL: An estate limited in the manner that it can be passed on to heirs. Property that cannot be sold but only transferred by inheritance.

FOLIO: A large sheet of paper folded in half to form the pages of a book. Or a book numbered only on one side of a full page.

FREEDOM RIGHT: An indentured servant's right to a specified amount of acreage at the end of his term of service.

FREEHOLD: An estate held outright with no other claims on it and which may be transferred to heirs or others.

FREEHOLDER: A person who owns property rather than rents that property.

FRIENDLY SOCIETY: A public business required to buy a permit or license, thus contributing to the community through indirect taxes.

GILD: A tax.

GLEBE: Land belonging to a parish or benefice given to the minister for his use during his ministry.

GOODS AND CHATTELS: Personal property. Goods usually meant inanimate objects, chattels were usually live stock.

GORE: A county subdivision in early Maine and Vermont.

<u>GRANT:</u> Property that is bestowed formally, as a privilege. To make conveyance of. To give the possession or title of, especially by deed or formal writing. To give a piece of property from a governing body.

<u>GRANTEE:</u> The buyer, purchaser, or receiver of real or personal property rights from the seller or the grantor, usually by deed or through a trust document.

<u>GRANTOR:</u> The seller, or person who sells, grants, transfers, or conveys real or personal property or property rights to the purchaser, usually by a deed or trust document.

<u>GREAT SURVEY:</u> Any of the 37 independent surveys conducted by the U.S. Government which established base lines and prim meridians creating 37 independent survey systems.

<u>GREAVE (also GRIEVE):</u> A bailiff, foreman, or sheriff.

<u>GUNTER'S CHAIN:</u> A unit of measurement by a surveyor (66 feet).

<u>*HABENDUM ET TENENDUM*:</u> A Latin term meaning to have and to hold to the Grantee (buyer or donor) his heirs and assigns. Clause in a deed that specifies the type of property or estate the buyer will receive.

<u>HEADRIGHT:</u> A document obtained by a person qualifying for a headright grant. (see next)

<u>HEADRIGHT GRANT:</u> A land grant system introduced to attract people to the colonies under which each head of family who emigrated to the colonies was given fifty acres of land providing he settle on it and improve the land and pay a fee to the crown.

<u>HEARTH TAX:</u> A tax begun in England based on the number of fireplaces in the home, unless exempted by poverty.

<u>HECTARE:</u> A metric measure of land equal to 10,000 square meters.

<u>HIDE OF LAND:</u> A land measurement which varied from 80 to 120 acres. It represented the amount of land that would support

a family, or as much land as could be plowed by one person in a year's time.

HOGSHEAD: A cask or barrel with the capacity of 60 to 140 gallons of liquid or 750 to 1,200 pounds of tobacco. May be used in the sale of land as a consideration.

HOME LOT: A plot of land where the home was built on a large farm including the area around the house and the enclosed fenced garden and feed lot for animals.

HOMESTEAD: The house and adjoining lands where the head of the family lives, which passes to the widow when her husband dies and is exempt from claims of creditors.

HOMESTEAD ACT: Any of the several legislative acts authorizing sale of public lands.

HOMESTEAD LANDS: Public lands disposed of through the Homestead Act process designated for the specific lands.

IMPRIMIS: A Latin term meaning in the first place, chiefly, or especially.

INDENTURE: An *Agreement* or *Deed* between two or more parties conveying real estates. Originally made in two parts that could be separated by tearing and matching a jagged line and matched later.

INDICTMENT: A document based on a decision by a grand jury that says sufficient evidence exists to bring a person to trial. Found in land and deed records when there is a disagreement.

INDIRECT TAX: A tax from sources other than property or income, such as a business, profession, entertainment, animals, etc. Sometimes found in more modern deeds mentioned when land is used as a business.

INDISCRIMINATE SURVEY: A survey not tied to any large survey grid, strictly speaking often incorrectly referred to as metes and bounds because it incorporated the use of compass bearings. When new surveys were made (more modern and accurate) the words indiscriminate survey may be used to justify the new measurement.

IN FEE SIMPLE: An absolute inheritance limited to a specific class of heirs.

IN LOT: A lot surveyed and platted within a new or established town.

INSTANT: Literally, the same as is given.

INTERMARRIAGE: The condition of a marriage contract being a reciprocal and mutual engagement by which each of the parties were married to the other. This has nothing to do with the parties being related to one another.

ISSUE: Lineal descendants of a common ancestor.

ITEM: A term used to mark the beginning of a paragraph.

JOINT TENANCY: Two or more persons owning a piece of property at the same time.

LAND GRANT ACT: An 1862 act which granted public land to the states to use for the establishing agricultural colleges.

LAND GRAVE: In South Carolina, one who owned 48,000 acres of land.

LAND MARKER: A stone, tree, stake, or any landmark used to mark a spot from which land measurements were made.

LAND JOBBER: One who buys land on speculation.

LAND WARRANT: A negotiable government certificate entitling the holder to be in possession of a designated amount of public land or other appropriation by the United States Congress.

LAPSED LAND: Land set aside to be claimed as bounty. Or land paid for but never claimed.

LEASE: A contract by which a landlord gives a tenant the use of lands, buildings, etc. for a specified time and for fixed payments.

LEASE AND RELEASE: A method of *buying* land to avoid paying the English Court fees in which the land was leased for a specified period until all rights were finally purchased through a release. This is the first time a legal deed was issued.

LESSEE: A person who leases land or property. (can be lessee of a slave)

LESSOR: The owner of property that is leased to another.

LETTERS PATENT: Title to land.

LIEN: A claim held by a person upon the property of another until a debt has been paid.

LIFE ESTATE: Ownership of property only during the life of the person holding title.

LINEAL: A direct line of descent.

LINK: A unit of measure - 7.92 inches, which is 1/100th of a chain used in measuring land.

LIS PENDENS: Notices of suits pending litigation, sometimes called equity notices. Usually these involve actions concerning real property such as mortgage foreclosures.

LIVERY: The legal delivery of property into the hands of the new owner.

MAJORITY: The age which one is no longer a minor, subject to local law.

MANSE: A parsonage or acreage large enough to support a family.

MASTER TITLE PLAT SYSTEM: Plats on which are shown survey data necessary to identify and describe public domain lands. The activity shown by the surveys indicate whether the availability of public lands and resources need to limited or restricted for use.

MEANDER LINE: In surveying, a traverse of the line of a permanent natural structure, such as a body of water.

MESNE CONVEYANCE: A deed which intervenes between the original grant and the deed held by the present owner. Some southern offices file these in a separate MESNE office.

METES AND BOUNDS: Surveying by natural, physical, and topographical features in conjunction with measurements and artificially designated objects or places. *Metes* refers to the measuring of direction and distance while *Bounds* refers to natural or man-made features of the land. (In states using this system of measurement to determine property lines, it is not unusual for the currant owner to have a bundle of documents relating to the *Document of Original Title.* These documents might be passed on to the new owner. The natural boundary lines may have changed through the years and this Document of Original Title may differ from the current boundaries.)

MILITARY LAND: Public land which was reserved as bounty land (or payment) for soldiers of the Revolutionary War and the War of 1812, as part of their compensation for service.

MILITARY WARRANT: A certificate – given to a veteran for claiming land as compensation for service. Especially in Kentucky, Ohio, and New York.

MOIETY: One half or equal share of anything.

MORE OR LESS: Approximately. Often counted in the rectangular survey system of land descriptions. This comes from the fact that all north-south range lines used to establish reference points in the survey system are not true north, causing some sections to contain less than 360 acres.

MORGAN: A Dutch measure of land, the amount one man or team of horses could plow in one morning (2 and 1/10th acres.)

MOVABLES: Personal property such as furniture, animals, food, clothing, etc. which can be carried from one place to another.

MUNIMENTS: Documents showing that a person has the legal rights to land, possessions, or other privileges.

MUNIMENTS OF TITLE: All written evidence of title which can show proof of ownership.

NEE: Used to identify a married woman by her maiden name.

NEXT FRIEND: One who acts on behalf of another if he cannot act for himself. Can be related or not.

NORTHWEST ORDINANCE OF 1785: A land act which provided public lands be surveyed and described with terms of township, range, section, and subsection used as descriptive terms.

OPEN FIELD: A system by which open farmland or pasture was divided among the villagers but not fenced off separately.

OUTSETTLER: One who made his home some distance from the main body of the town or village.

PACE: A measure of distance equal to 2 and 1/2 to 3 feet.

PARCEL: A piece of land with definite boundaries and a specific description.

PARENT COUNTY: The county from which a new one was formed.

PARISHING: A hamlet or small village belonging to a parish.

PARTITION: A division of land when two or more persons hold real estate as co-tenants and then each of them take separate parts.

PARTITION OF SUCCESSION: A division of effects in which a succession is composed among all coheirs according to their respective rights which may be voluntary or judicial.

PATENT: A grant made by a government to an individual, conveying fee simple title to Public Lands. The official document of such a grant. The land is *granted.*

PATENTEE: One who receives a grant of land by way of a patent.

PECULIAR: A piece of land not incorporated into a township.

PERCH: A unit of land measurement equal to a rod or pole (16.5 feet or 5.5 yards).

PLAT: A small piece of land. Or a *map* of these small pieces of land.

PLAT OF SURVEY: A drawing showing boundaries, divisions, and other features of a piece of land.

POLES: Measurement of the land using the survey system: 1 square pole equal 1 square chain.

PRAEDIAL LAND: Property attached to land, such as slaves, issuing or coming from the land.

PRE-EMPTION LANDS: Public lands granted by another sovereign.

PRESCRIPTION: The right to use a particular piece of land. A right or title through possession and continual use.

PRESENTS: Used in legal documents to indicate the document in which the phrase is mentioned. " By these presents" means the document.

PRIMOGENITURE: The *exclusive* right of the firstborn male to inherit property from the parents is no longer used in the United States. It was used until about the time of the Articles of Confederation. During the time it was used in this country it was not always enforced, but should be considered when searching.

PRINCIPAL MERIDIAN: The first or beginning North-South running line laid out in each of the 37 different surveys of public domain states as measurement.

PROCESSION: The process of reestablishing land ownership boundaries by physically waling these lines in the company of an appointed processioner and the owners of the adjoining lands.

PROOF OF RESIDENCE: The paperwork verifying length or time of residency.

PRO TEMPORE: A Latin term meaning "temporarily."

PROTHONOTARY: The chief notary or law clerk within a county.

QUIT CLAIM DEED: A deed releasing claim to an estate of property by an individual to another individual.

QUIT RENT FEE: In early Virginia, an annual fee paid to the King in exchange for the right to live on the farm or property. This land was usually later claimed and purchased by the payee.

RANGE: An area between range lines (the North-South running lines) as a part of the Rectangular Survey System. Together with township lines (East-West running lines), range lines form areas of 6 miles square or 36 miles called Townships.

REAL PROPERTY: Land and permanent attachments including buildings, timber, crops, etc., as well as the right to issue the ownership of lands.

REALTY: Land and tenements.

RECTANGULAR SURVEY SYSTEM OF 1785: A method, passed by the Continental Congress which divided Public Land States into 37 separate survey systems, each separate survey consisting of a starting point, and East-West running base line, and a North-South running principle meridian.

RELICT: A widow or widower. The surviving spouse.

RELINQUISHMENT LAND: Land sold without title to its minerals, which remained vested in the State.

RIGHT: A document which established a person's right to lands which were issued to the county surveyor which allowed him to survey the land desired by the potential patentee.

RIPARIAN: A person who lives on the banks of the river or near the water.

ROD: A unit of measurement equal to one pole or perch (16.5 feet or 5.5 yards).

ROOD: A unit of measurement equal to 1/4 acre (40 square rods) or the length of 5.5 to 8 yards.

SECTION: A measurement of land used in the Rectangular Survey System which equals 640 acres or one square mile.

SEISIN (also SEIZIN): A freehold (held in fee simple or for life) estate. At one time land could only be held in seisin, because all land was owned by a reigning sovereign (King).

SHARECROPPER: A person who would farm land owned by another and divide the crops or profits with the owner on an agreed basis.

SIC: A Latin word meaning *thus*. Used to show that a quoted passage is precisely reproduced.

SITIO: A land measurement or league equal to 4,428 acres.

SOCAGE: A system of land tenure by which a tenant could live on and work the land in return for services given to a Lord that were not military in nature. When this service was honorable it was called *free socage*, but if it was considered base, it was called *villein socage*.

SOUTHWEST TERRITORY: A region in 1790, officially known as the Territory of the United States south of the Ohio River.

SPECULATOR: One who bought and sold lands (usually for profit).

SQUATTER: A person who settles on public land or the property of another without claim or title, or who cannot gain title to land no matter how long he has occupied the land.

STATE: To deed land to a person. To survey and build a road between two points.

STATUS PLAT: A copy of a plat map or survey containing the necessary information to determine federal ownership of public lands and resources.

STEWARD: A person entrusted with the care and management of anothers estate or household.

SURVEY PLAT: A map on which land surveys are recorded at a scale of two inches per mile. Each plat usually shows one township. Property measurements and names may be recorded on Survey or Plat Maps. They may show relationships, locations of parents and children, and other information. Land may have been divided between several children at the death of a parent.

> Survey plats may contain information such as: "17 poles to the corner of Richard Lee's land, thence 22 poles to the white oak, thence 14 poles to the corner of John Lee's lane, thence ..." From this description, we should be led to see who John and Richard Lee are? Are they relatives? Were they grandmother's brother, father or uncle? Close proximity does not always indicate relationships, but it often does and should be investigated.

SURVEYOR'S MEASURE: A length of chain (gunter's chain) measuring 66 feet.

TACT: Tenure or tenancy on land.

TENANCY AT WILL: As long as the landlord or tenant wish to continue their arrangement can be called Tenancy at Will.

TENANCY BY THE ENTIRETY: Husband and wife together in which on the death of one the entire interest in the property diverts to the other.

TENANT: A name used for indentured servants who were settled on farms, supplied tools, and engaged to remain on the land for specific noted years. One who holds property ownership or lives on the land, leasing or renting.

TENURE: The right to hold and use property and rents accrued from the property for an established period of time.

<u>TITLE:</u> Evidence of ownership.

<u>TOWNSHIP:</u> 6 square miles, 36 sections in Public Domain States.

<u>TRACT BOOK:</u> A log or book which is an index to and digest of all essential actions which affect public lands.

<u>WARRANT:</u> A statement which denotes that the seller has clear title and will defend said title.

<u>WARRANTY DEED:</u> A deed whereby one which includes a covenant by the seller to defend the title and possession of the estate granted.

<u>YEOMAN:</u> A freeholder who works his own estate.